# Christmas for

## Merry Christmas

Merry Christmas everyone
Upon this blessed day;
I hope that every happiness
Will always come your way.
And as the Christmas bells ring out
If you have joy to spare,
Just open up your heart and door
That others, too, might share.
For at this happy time of year
It's love that brings the Christ Child near.

Carice Williams

**Editorial Director,** James Kuse
**Managing Editor,** Ralph Luedtke
**Photographic Editor,** Gerald Koser
**Production Editor,** Stuart L. Zyduck

**designed by** Jan Frances Engel

**artwork by** Miki Ferro
and
Lorraine Wells

ISBN 0-89542-450-9 225

# Christmas Story

Let me tell you a beautiful story,
Though I know you have heard it before,
As the years roll on into centuries
The story is told o'er and o'er,
And each time the tale is repeated
Its beauty increases the more.

One night, in a far eastern country,
While shepherds were watching their sheep,
With the stillness of night all around them
(For most of the world lay asleep),
An angel appeared and a bright star
Shone down from the heavenly deep.

"Fear not, for I bring you good tidings
Of great joy!" the angel said.
Then he told of the Babe sent from Heaven
Who lay in a crude cattle shed,
And the shepherds followed the bright star
Till they came to His humble bed.

And a mighty choir of angels
Burst forth into singing then,
The beautiful theme of their anthem
Repeated again and again,
"Glory to God in the highest,
Peace on earth, good will to men!"

Three wise men sought and found Him
And worshiped the Babe where He lay,
And they brought their richest treasures
To the Prince of Peace that day:
Pure gold, frankincense and myrrh
For a Child on a bed of hay.

There's joy in the Christmas story,
Today as in ages past;
And for those who love the Christ Child
And by faith still hold Him fast,
There's a better world in the offing
And the promise of peace at last.

Alice Seward

# The Little Star

Once upon a time God created the heaven and the earth. On the first day God said, "Let there be light," and He placed all the stars in the sky—all but one.

This little star was hurt; and it began to cry because God had not given it a chance to shine like the others. But when the little star went to Him and asked why, God replied, "Little star, you must grow some more before I can use you."

Many years went by. Then, down on earth one day, God's favorite people, the Israelites, escaped from their bondage in Egypt. Their leader was a man named Moses, and he led the people between the walls of the river on toward the land of Canaan.

And God said, "I need three million stars to form a pillar of fire, to lead my children to the promised land. Who will volunteer?" The little star thought, "now is my chance to shine —I'll volunteer." But when it came before God, He shook His head and told it, "Not yet, little star; you must become brighter before I can use you."

Faster and faster the years passed. All the while the little star was growing larger and brighter. "When will my time come?" it wondered.

On the nights when the clouds hid the other stars from earth, the little star tried to steal beneath the clouds and light the way of the travelers who were lost and could not find their paths home. But each time, God would stop it, saying, "I am not ready to use you, little star; have patience and some day I will give you your chance."

"How much I am missing," the little star complained as it watched the bigger stars keeping their vigil over

David as he slept in the fields at night. "How I, too, would love to inspire the poets to write their Psalms as do the other stars." Centuries rolled past without a chance for the little star to shine; but all the while it was growing larger and brighter.

Then one day, God called to it, "Little star, the time has come; I am ready to use you."

The little star began to twinkle with anticipation; what did God have in store for it? As it beamed with satisfaction, God took the little star in His hand, and placed it in the sky. "Now, shine little star," God said. And shine it did!

While the little star was shining it noticed that three Wise Men were looking at it with exceeding joy, as if it held the answer to some question in their minds. Strange to say, the little star felt that it must lead them somewhere. It began to move, and wherever it went, the Wise Men followed.

As it glided across the sky, the little star noticed that it was headed for a town that lay in the distance. The closer it came to the village, the brighter it beamed. When it reached the edge of the town, the little star burst forth into a radiance which was much more beautiful than any other star had ever possessed.

Suddenly it stopped directly over a stable. And as it hovered there, the three Wise Men stepped down from their camels and hurried into the stable.

"What are they looking for?" the little star pondered. From the heavens it heard God's reply, "This is my beloved Son, in whom I am well pleased."

Suddenly, a wonderful peace came over the little star. It knew that soon God would call it out of the sky for its task was done. But it was happy. It had served its purpose and was ready to give way to a greater Light—a Light which was the life of men.

Richard Blanchard

# A Legend

There's a beautiful legend
That's never been told—
It may have been known
To the Wise Men of old—
How three little children
Came early at dawn,
With hearts that were sad,
To where Jesus was born.

One could not see,
One was too lame to play,
While the other, a mute,
Not a word could he say.

Yet, led by His star,
They came there to peep
At the little Lord Jesus
With eyes closed in sleep.

But how could the Christ Child,
So lovely and fair,
Not waken and smile
When He heard their glad prayer
Of hope at His coming,
Of faith in His birth,
Of praise at His bringing
God's peace to the earth?

And, then, as the light
Softly came through the door,
The lad that was lame
Stood upright once more.
The boy that was mute
Started sweetly to sing,
While the child that was blind
Looked with joy on the King!

Author Unknown

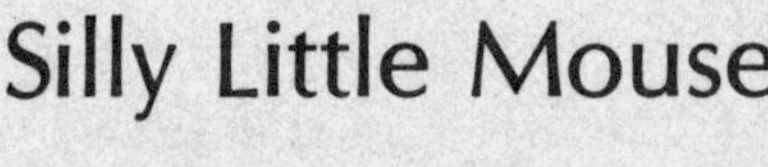

# Silly Little Mouse

Once, when it was Christmas Eve,
 A silly little mouse
Tried to stay awake to see
 Santa in his house.

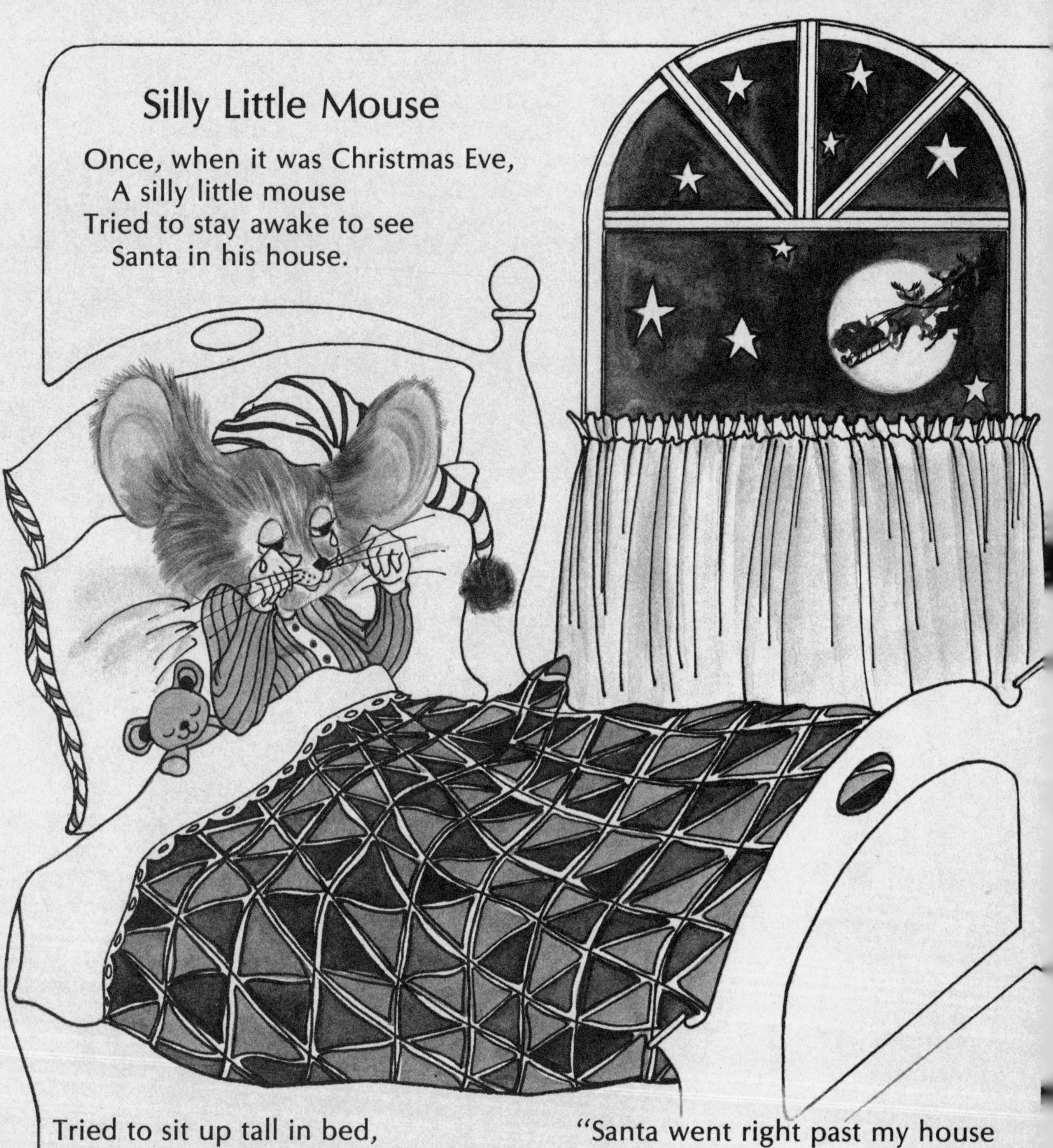

Tried to sit up tall in bed,
 Piled his pillows high,
Watched the stars, like Christmas lights
 Strung across the sky.

Listened for the sound of bells—
 Thought he heard them near,
Thought he heard them go away!
 Sobbed, "Oh dear, oh dear—

"Santa went right past my house
 And he didn't stop!"
Thought his little heart would break
 Spilled two tears, plip-plop.

Wished that he had gone to sleep,
 Closed his little eyes—
Woke up in the morning, and—
 What a fine surprise!

Here were little toys galore
And a Christmas tree—
There his little stocking hung,
Full as it could be!

Danced around his little tree,
Drummed his little drum,
"Oh," he cried, "how can this be?
Santa Claus did come.

"I was sure I heard him go
Sailing through the sky—
I was sure he never stopped—
Sure he went right by!

"Did he know I was awake?
Hear my eyelids blink?
Did he hear my whiskers twitch?
Did he laugh and wink?

"Did he go clear round the world
And come back to my house
After I was sound asleep—
Me, a little mouse?"

Kathryn Jackson

## Song

Why do the bells of Christmas ring?
Why do little children sing?
Once a lovely shining star,
Seen by shepherds from afar,
Gently moved until its light
Made a manger's cradle bright.

There a darling baby lay,
Pillowed soft upon the hay,
And its mother sang and smiled:
"This is Christ, the Holy Child!"
Therefore bells for Christmas ring,
Therefore little children sing.

Eugene Field

## What Can I Give Him?

What can I give Him,
  Poor as I am?
If I were a shepherd
  I would give Him a lamb,

If I were a Wise Man,
  I would do my part,
But what can I give Him,
  Give my heart.

Christina G. Rossetti

# Christmas

Christmas is a silver star
That shone on Bethlehem,
Where lay the baby Jesus
Sent to save all men.

Christmas is a feeling
Of happiness and prayer
In every home, in every heart,
With power rich and rare.

Christmas is a story
And the carols that we sing,
The bells that ring merrily,
And snowflakes on the wing.

Christmas is a greeting card,
The handclasp of a friend,
The splendor of an evergreen,
A magic without end.

Christmas is a package
Wrapped in ribbons bright,
And mistletoe and holly,
And candles shedding light.

Christmas is a lovely feast
Prepared for one and all
And happy golden memories
So pleasant to recall.

Christmas is the whole world
Joined, in peace and love,
For everlasting brotherhood
And blessings from above.

LaVerne P. Larson

# Susie's Christmas Star

Once there was a little girl who saved and saved her pennies to buy a new star for the top of the Christmas tree.

Her name was Susie, and she said to her family, "It was my kitten that tore up the old star—so it's up to me to get a new one!"

So she saved and she saved; and by Christmas Eve, Susie had a pocketful of pennies for buying a star. When the tree was all trimmed (except for the star) and shining in the front window, Susie hurried into her snow clothes.

"Now just wait till I get back!" she said.

Then she whisked out into the snow and down to the paper store.

She chose a most beautiful, shining star. And when she had paid for it, Susie had lots and lots of pennies left over.

Now who wants to have pennies left over on Christmas Eve?

Not Susie!

She looked at the rows of candy canes hanging on a wire across the store—big ones, middle-sized ones, and little ones.

And soon Susie was on her way out the door, carrying a big bag full of little candy canes, with the shining star on top. But just as the door closed, its wet, snowy edge rubbed the bag and tore a hole in one corner.

Now Susie never saw that. She was much too busy thinking how surprised her family would be when she opened the bag. She hurried up the snowy street, slipping and sliding and leaving a trail of candy canes behind her.

By the time she came to the second lamppost from home, the bag felt very light. Susie peeped in, and looked in, and stared in—and there was nothing left in the bag but the star and a big, dampish hole.

"The canes!" she cried. "I've lost the candy canes!" And she whirled around and went down the street looking and looking in the snow.

At last she did see a hole such as a candy cane might make. But there was no cane in it. It was just a hole with Susie's footprint beside it and another footprint going the other way.

So with all the other holes in the snow. Just holes, with footprints beside them.

"Somebody found my canes!" whispered Susie. "Somebody took them home—and I'll just follow the footprints, and find the house, and knock on the door and say, 'Please give me back my candy canes!'"

Susie followed those footprints past the store, which was all closed

and dark by now, and past a vacant lot, and past a junkyard—

—and straight to a small house with a tiny yard and a sagging porch.

She didn't go up on the porch. She tiptoed to the window first, because when you are going to knock on a door and say, 'Please give me back my candy canes!" it's well to be sure the canes are there.

And when Susie looked in that window, she saw a small room with a mother in it, and a baby, and a little boy, just about her own size.

There was a little tree in the room, too. It was a small, thin tree, and it had nothing on it but candles, and all of Susie's candy canes.

"Every single one!" she whispered.

She was just about to go to the door when the mother lighted the candles and smiled the happiest kind of smile. The baby clapped its hands. And the little boy capered around the tree looking so proud and happy that Susie stood still.

"Maybe," she thought, "maybe I

don't need those canes, after all—"

And just as Susie thought that, the little boy stopped capering. He stood and looked at the tree; and he said, "Now, if we only had a star for the top—oh, wouldn't it be the most beautiful tree in the world?"

Susie heard that, because the window was a little bit open. Just the littlest bit—just enough for hearing and just enough for pushing something through.

"Just enough," thought Susie, reaching into the bag. She took out the beautiful, shining star, and she pushed it through the window.

And when she had, Susie turned around and went running home just as fast as she could go.

She whisked into her house with the empty bag.

"Well," smiled her daddy, "we waited, Susie."

"We waited a long time!" cried her brothers and sisters, crowding around her. "And now show us the new star!"

"There is no star," said Susie. "No candy canes, either—"

She told her family everything that had happened. And when she came to the part about pushing the Christmas star through the window, she hung her head.

"So now," she said, "now there's no star at all for the top of our tree!"

And she looked so sad that her mother and daddy and all her sisters and brothers hugged her and said, "Never mind, Susie! Never mind a bit. You did the rightest kind of thing—and our tree is just beautiful anyway!"

Then they all turned to look at the beautiful, shining tree that filled the whole wide window with its spreading branches.

They all looked up at the bare spot at the top—halfway up the topmost pane—

And do you know—

—on the topmost branch there was a star.

It was a real star, the biggest and brightest in the whole dark Christmas Eve sky; and it was shining through the window, just as if someone had put it right smack on top of the tree especially for Susie!"

Kathryn Jackson

# The First Christmas Tree

This story of the First Christmas Tree was told me by the Fairy Queen herself, so you may be quite sure it is a true one. Here it is.

Once upon a time there lived in the middle of a forest a poor woodcutter.

He had one little daughter called Annis, whom he loved dearly. Annis was a dear little girl, kind and gentle.

She was very fond of all the woodland creatures, and they in turn knew and loved her well. The fairies loved her also. They used to dance on the top of the low stone wall that went around the little garden in front of the cottage.

"Annis! Annis!" they would call to her while she was busy helping her mother in the kitchen. But she would shake her head.

"I can't come. I'm busy," she would answer.

But at nighttime, when she was fast asleep under her red quilt, they would come tapping at the little window.

"Annis! Annis!"

Then she would slip out of bed and run quickly downstairs with her bare feet, and off with the fairies into the moon-shining woods.

But the next day she was never sure whether it had been a dream or reality.

That was in the summer. It was winter now and very cold. The sky was dark and heavy with coming snow.

Every evening, all through the winter, Annis would hang a little lantern with a candle in it on the small fir tree that grew just inside the garden gate. Her father could see it as he came home through the trees. It was a little bright welcome for him even before he reached home.

On Christmas Eve, he went to work as usual. He came home for his dinner at midday and started back early. He was at work quite a long way off.

"I shall finish there today," he said to his wife as he left the house.

"Then I shall come nearer home. If the snow comes, it will be difficult to find the way in the dark evenings."

And that very day the snow began. All the afternoon it fell in great, soft flakes.

Down, down, down—it seemed as if the whole sky were falling in little bits.

The woodcutter worked hard in the fading light.

It was quite dark by the time he had finished, and he had to keep shaking the snow from his shoulders and from his old hat.

The wood was all neatly stacked in the little shed which had been built up there to house it.

He started off home with a sigh of relief, smiling to himself as he thought of his warm hearth and the bowl of hot porridge waiting for him on the hob, and of little Annis knitting in the chimney corner.

But presently—how it happened I know not for he knew the forest well, and the snow had almost stopped falling, and the moon was shining—he found that he had lost his way.

He was quite cheerful at first. "In a minute I shall find the path again," he said. But many minutes passed and he did not find it. A cloud came over the moon; the snow began to fall again more thickly. It was like a moving, whirling mist where the trees stood less close together.

The woodcutter began to lose heart. Then, suddenly, he saw a light ahead of him on one of the fir trees.

"Can I be so near home?" he said, half-bewildered. But when he came near he found that it was not a fir tree in his own garden that was lit up, but an ordinary forest tree. Little lights twinkled and glittered on its branches, burning brightly and steadily in spite of the falling snow. The woodcutter rubbed his eyes. "If this be wicked magic," he thought, "it will now disappear." But the lights burned more brightly than ever, and as he looked about he saw in the distance another tree lit up in the same way. Then he understood.

"It is the good fairies helping me," he said, and trudged off cheerily in the direction of the second tree.

And when he looked back, the first one had already grown dark again. But when he reached the second tree, another was shining ahead to show him the way.

And so he went on from tree to tree until at last he was guided safely home to Annis' little lantern in his own garden.

And always after that, he used to put lights on a little fir tree on Christmas Eve in memory of the time when the fairies saved him from being lost in the forest. And so the custom began, and because it was such a pretty one, and because the fairies so willed it, it spread; and today the fairy Christmas tree is to be found all over the world in houses where there are children and where the fairies come.

Rose Fyleman

MIKI

# Sly Santa Claus

All the house was asleep
And the fire burning low,
When, from far up the chimney
Came down a "Ho! ho!"
And a little, round man,
With a terrible scratching,
Dropped into the room
With a wink that was catching.
Yes, down he came, bumping,
And thumping, and jumping,
And picking himself up without a sign of a bruise!

"Ho! ho!" he kept on,
As if bursting with cheer.
"Good children, gay children,
Glad children, see here!
I have brought you fine dolls,
And gay trumpets, and rings,
Noah's arks, and bright skates,
And a host of good things!
I have brought a whole sackful,
A packful, a backful!
Come hither, come hither, come hither and choose!

"Ho! ho! What is this?
Why, they all are asleep!
But their stockings are up
And my presents will keep!
So, in with the candies,
The books, and the toys;
All the goodies I have
For the good girls and boys.
I'll ram them, and jam them,
And slam them, and cram them;
All the stockings will hold while the tired youngsters snooze."

All the while his round shoulders
Kept ducking and ducking;
And his little, fat fingers
Kept tucking and tucking;
Until every stocking
Bulged out on the wall
As if it were bursting
And ready to fall.
And then, all at once,
With a whisk and a whistle,
And twisting himself
Like a tough bit of gristle,
He bounced up again
Like the down of a thistle,
And nothing was left but the prints of his shoes.

Mrs. C. S. Stone

MIKI

# A Child's Faith

"He slept in a manger;
He had no bed."
"I would have given
Him mine," she said.

"He walked alone
On the shores of Galilee."
"I wish He were here;
He could walk with me."

Such is a child's heart,
Full of love and peace;
Small wonder He said,
"Become such as these."

Christie Lund Coles

# The Christ Child and the Pine Tree

The lights on the Christmas tree have always been symbolic of the stars. There is a story that tells why they are used on the Christmas tree.

When Christ was born in Bethlehem not only did the shepherds and the Wise Men come to honor the young Child, but birds, beasts and plants, too, came to offer gifts. Each one had something of his own to offer the Babe. That is, all except one. That one was the pine tree. It had nothing to offer but its needles, and they would only prick the Baby and were not at all suitable.

But God saw how disappointed the little tree was, so he told some of the stars to go down and rest on its branches. When they did, the little tree was covered with such radiance that the Child saw it and stretched His arms toward it in happiness.

From that time forth at Christmastime, the little pine tree always bears lights in memory of the night it gave pleasure to the Christ Child.

Elizabeth Hough Sechrist and Janette Woolsey

# The Friendly Beasts

Jesus, our brother, strong and good,
Was humbly born in a stable rude;
And the friendly beasts around Him stood,
Jesus, our brother, strong and good.

"I" said the donkey, shaggy and brown,
"I carried His mother up hill and down;
I carried her safely to Bethlehem town;
I," said the donkey, shaggy and brown.

"I," said the cow, all white and red,
"I gave Him my manger for His bed;
I gave Him my hay to pillow His head;
I," said the cow, all white and red.

"I," said the sheep with curly horn,
"I gave Him my wool for His blanket warm;
He wore my coat on Christmas morn;
I," said the sheep with curly horn.

"I," said the dove, from the rafters high,
"Cooed Him to sleep, my mate and I;
We cooed Him to sleep, my mate and I;
I," said the dove, from the rafters high.

And every beast, by some good spell,
In the stable dark was glad to tell
Of the gift he gave Emmanuel,
The gift he gave Emmanuel.

Twelfth Century Carol

# Jesus, My Shepherd

Dear Jesus, I am still too small
To really understand;
Please let me put my tiny heart
In Your beloved hand.

I want to be the little lamb
That nestles in Your arms,
Away from sin and sadness and
From everything that harms.

I never want to leave Your side
For any kind of play,
Because You are so good to me
Each moment of the day.

I know You are my Father in
The Heaven of my dreams,
Where everything is beautiful
And happy as it seems.

Dear Jesus, be my Shepherd now
Protect and comfort me,
And let me be Your little lamb
For all eternity.

James J. Metcalfe

# The Carol That Never Was Sung

The first Christmas Eve, of course, was a very important event. The birthday of the Child called for the biggest celebration the heavenly hosts had ever had. Even the Carols, held in reserve for ages for some really special event, would be sung.

The choir was to be one of Heaven's very best, with some exceptionally rich angelic tenors and basses brought in from the glee club to help out. All the stars had been rubbed with a special polish, and one brand-new star added just for the occasion. The Carols were quite puffed up with pride and excitement, and they all promised solemnly to be on hand in plenty of time.

On the great night, everything went off fine. The stars shone as they had never shone before; the angel choir outdid itself in paeans of joy and the Carols were a great success. There was only one little flaw, and hardly anyone even noticed it. One of the Carols didn't get there in time.

In fact, it didn't get there at all.

It was quite a sweet Carol, the angel singers told each other a little sadly. It had been a pity not to have sung it.

The Carol was very penitent. It had stopped on the way, it explained vaguely. Something had got its attention, and it had stopped and been late. Questioning by the choirmaster produced little more. The Carol got vaguer and vaguer as the questions became sharper and sharper. Only one thing it seemed sure about.

It would never happen again, the Carol promised.

But it did, every year. And finally, when nearly twenty long centuries had gone by with the last Carol still not sung, they brought the situation to the Throne Room. There they explained, more in sorrow than in anger, about the Carol that was always late.

Then, at a sign, they left; and the Last Carol was summoned. The Last Carol was ashamed and frightened and hung its head as it stood in the Throne Room and explained with no more vagueness why it had been late.

Each year had been something different, it admitted. Sometimes it had been a man in a dungeon. Often it had been men and women whose spirits had fallen low in the face of great obstacles, whose faith in love was almost extinguished and who could not join in the rejoicing over the Child's birthday.

Always, explained the Carols simply, it had seemed important to stop with these for awhile; and somehow it had always meant being late. "But next year . . . " began the Carol. But the Voice from the Throne interrupted.

"Next year," said the Voice, "you will do as you have done. Next year and for many years to come. For you are the Carol that must be voiceless until all men sing together in a mighty chorus that covers the earth. Only in the hearts of men who have seen the vision," said the voice, "can you honor the Child, until all men love each other as He loved them."

"Then," said the Carol wistfully, "must I be silent forever?"

"Not so," said the Voice; and the full choir of angels had never sounded so richly majestic. "They flee from it in fear and greed, but with their fear there is shame, and through their greed shines love. One day they will cast out their fears and let love lead them into the rich habitation I have prepared for them. Then," said the Voice, "all men will join in singing the sweetest carol of all . . . the song of universal brotherhood."

Alfred Hassler

Dear Lord, as I look up at the stars
on this very special day,
I wonder what the Wise Men thought
as they traveled on their way.
I think of baby Jesus, and the manger where He lay,
and hope that He will guide me
As I live through every day!

Jeanne Veit

## I'm Glad That I Believe

A lot of folks are skeptical,
Their minds just filled with doubt;
They wonder how our Santa Claus
Just ever gets about.
And is it true he brings his gifts
And comes on Christmas Eve?
Whatever else the others think,
I'm glad that I believe.

I know that in the years gone by,
He brought those lovely toys.
I'm certain that he knows and loves
All little girls and boys;
And I, for one, shall be so good
From now till Christmas Eve,
And there's not one can change my mind.
I'm glad that I believe.

Garnett Ann Schultz

*ACKNOWLEDGMENTS*

*SONG by Eugene Field. From COMPLETE POEMS by Eugene Field. (Charles Scribner's Sons, 1901). THE CAROL THAT NEVER WAS SUNG by Alfred Hassler. Used by permission of Fellowship of Reconciliation, Nyack, New York. JESUS, MY SHEPHERD by James J. Metcalfe. Copyrighted. Courtesy Field Enterprises, Inc. Our sincere thanks to the following authors whose addresses we were unable to locate: Mrs. C. S. Stone for SLY SANTA CLAUS; Elizabeth Hough Sechrist and Janette Woolsey for THE CHRIST CHILD AND THE PINE TREE from IT'S TIME FOR CHRISTMAS, written and compiled by Elizabeth Hough Sechrist and Janette Woolsey, Copyright © 1959, by Elizabeth Hough Sechrist and Janette Woolsey.*